March On!

Lucy Lang & Grace Lang

You've asked, my darling, about the women you see marching and talking about equality.

We come by
it honest,
it's our legacy,

from the grandmas who came before even me.

Those great-great-grandmas,
because they were ladies,

couldn't choose their president,
or if to have babies.

There was no doubt that this just wouldn't do, so they planned a march down Fifth Avenue.

Thousands of women, a five mile parade!

My darling, it's how
great change gets made.

They came
by carriage,
they came
by horse,

**and some just walked
with their mothers, of course.**

Festooned with garlands
that looked so pretty,

a peaceful army
swept New York City!

There was more to
be done before
ballots were cast,
until all women,
by law, would be
equal at last.

For women of
color it took
still more years,
and there's more
work ahead,
so I'm glad that
you're here.

It's a century later, but if you ever feel small, just remember the moxie of those who stand tall.

Because democracy grants you permission to fight. Now close your eyes, my darling, sleep tight.

When America was founded, only white men were allowed to vote. In 1870, the law changed, giving black men the right to vote. However, racial discrimination kept them from exercising this right. On October 23, 1915, more than 25,000 women marched down New York City's Fifth Avenue to fight for women's right to vote. At the time it was the largest march in the city's history. In 1920, the 19th Amendment was added to the Constitution, giving women the right to vote. Unfortunately, women of color were still barred from voting. In 1924, indigenous people were given voting rights. It wasn't until many years later, in 1965, that the law changed once again – this time, granting men and women of color the legal protections they needed to vote.

Today, obstacles still prevent many Americans from voting – and women and others must keep marching on!

Dedicated in loving memory of Theresa Lang and Eldora Miller
and in adoring honor of Kristina Lang, Jane Lang,
Theresa Lang Asher, Tai Vardi Lang and Breanna Mosley Lang